Best of Malta

Top Spots to Explore

4

Intro

Welcome to the enchanting archipelago of Malta, where history whispers through the ancient limestone walls, and the azure Mediterranean sea sparkles under the Maltese sun. As you embark on your journey through this captivating land, allow me to be your guide through the tapestry of experiences awaiting you.

Nestled in the heart of the Mediterranean, Malta is a small but mighty gem, brimming with an illustrious past that dates back millennia. From the prehistoric temples that stand as silent sentinels to the grandeur of the Knights of St. John, each cobblestone street and sun-kissed shore holds a story waiting to be uncovered.

But Malta is more than just a living museum of history. It's a vibrant tapestry of cultures, where the echoes of Phoenician, Roman, Arab, and European influences blend seamlessly into the fabric of everyday life. From the bustling markets of Valletta to the quaint fishing villages of Marsaxlokk, the spirit of Malta is as diverse as its landscape.

And speaking of landscapes, prepare to be enchanted by the natural wonders that dot this island paradise. From the rugged cliffs of Dingli to the pristine beaches of Golden Bay, Malta's scenery is as diverse as it is breathtaking. Whether you're exploring the crystal-clear waters of the Blue Grotto or wandering through the lush gardens of San Anton, every corner of Malta offers a new perspective on the beauty of nature.

But perhaps the true magic of Malta lies in its people. Warm and welcoming, the Maltese are known for their hospitality and their love of life. Whether you're sharing a meal of freshly-caught seafood with locals in a seaside taverna or sipping on a glass of locally-produced wine under the stars, you'll find that the true essence of Malta lies in the connections you make with its people.

So, as you prepare to embark on your journey through the best that Malta has to offer, allow yourself to be swept away by the magic of this timeless land. From its ancient history to its vibrant culture, there's something here for everyone to discover and enjoy. Welcome to Malta - where every moment is an adventure waiting to be lived.

Valletta: Jewel of the Mediterranean

Welcome to Valletta, the radiant jewel of the Mediterranean and the proud capital of Malta. As you step into this UNESCO World Heritage city, prepare to be transported back in time to an era of grandeur and glory.

Named after the revered Grand Master of the Order of St. John, Jean Parisot de la Valette, who defended the island against the Ottoman siege in 1565, Valletta stands as a testament to Malta's rich and storied history. Designed by the famed military architect Francesco Laparelli, the city is a masterpiece of Baroque architecture, with its honey-hued buildings and imposing fortifications rising proudly against the backdrop of the sparkling sea.

Begin your journey through Valletta by wandering through its maze-like streets, where every corner reveals a new marvel waiting to be discovered. Marvel at the grand facades of the Auberge de Castille and the Grand Master's Palace, where the echoes of centuries past still linger in the air. Lose yourself in the bustling markets of Merchant Street, where artisans ply their trade amidst a symphony of sights, sounds, and scents.

But Valletta is not just a city frozen in time - it's a vibrant hub of culture and creativity, where history meets modernity in perfect harmony. Explore the cutting-edge galleries of the Valletta Contemporary, where local and international artists showcase their talents against the backdrop of ancient stone walls. Immerse yourself in the sounds of the Malta Philharmonic Orchestra as they perform in the majestic setting of the Manoel Theatre, one of Europe's oldest working theatres.

And no visit to Valletta would be complete without experiencing its culinary delights. From traditional Maltese delicacies like rabbit stew and pastizzi to international fusion cuisine served in chic waterfront restaurants, the city's dining scene is as diverse as it is delicious. And be sure to raise a glass of locally-produced wine or craft beer as you toast to the beauty and bounty of this extraordinary city.

So, whether you're wandering through its historic streets, immersing yourself in its cultural treasures, or savouring its culinary delights, Valletta is sure to capture your heart and ignite your imagination. Welcome to Valletta - where the past meets the present in a symphony of sights, sounds, and sensations unlike any other.

Mdina: The Silent City

Welcome to Mdina, the enchanting "Silent City" of Malta, where time seems to stand still amidst the labyrinthine streets of this ancient fortress town. Nestled atop a hill in the heart of the island, Mdina is a living testament to Malta's rich and diverse history.

As you pass through the imposing city gates and step into Mdina's timeless embrace, prepare to be transported back in time to a world of knights and nobility, where every cobblestone whispers tales of centuries past. Originally founded by the Phoenicians in around the 8th century BC, Mdina has been shaped by a succession of rulers, from the Romans to the Arabs to the Knights of St. John, each leaving their indelible mark on the city's architecture and culture.

Wander through Mdina's narrow streets, where graceful palaces and noble mansions stand as silent sentinels to a bygone era of splendour and intrigue. Admire the intricate Baroque facades of the Palazzo Falson and the Palazzo Santa Sofia, where the echoes of grandeur still linger in the air. Lose yourself in the tranquil beauty of St. Paul's Cathedral, with its stunning frescoes and majestic dome reaching towards the heavens.

But Mdina is not just a city frozen in time - it's a vibrant hub of culture and creativity, where history meets modernity in perfect harmony. Explore the charming boutiques and artisanal workshops that line its streets, where local craftsmen ply their trade amidst a backdrop of ancient stone walls. Indulge in the culinary delights of Mdina's quaint cafes and restaurants, where traditional Maltese dishes are served with a modern twist.

And as the sun sets over the shimmering Mediterranean sea, take a moment to pause and reflect on the timeless beauty of Mdina, where the past and present converge in a symphony of sights, sounds, and sensations unlike any other. Welcome to Mdina - where history comes alive in every stone, and the spirit of Malta shines bright.

Gozo: Island Escapades

Welcome to Gozo, the picturesque island paradise that beckons with its idyllic landscapes and timeless charm. Nestled just a short ferry ride away from the bustling streets of Malta, Gozo offers a tranquil retreat from the hustle and bustle of modern life.

As you step off the ferry and onto Gozo's shores, you'll immediately be struck by the island's natural beauty. From the rugged cliffs of Dwerja to the sandy beaches of Ramla Bay, Gozo's coastline is a patchwork of stunning vistas waiting to be explored. Whether you're diving into the crystal-clear waters of the Blue Hole or soaking up the sun on the golden sands of Marsalforn, Gozo's beaches offer a slice of paradise for every traveller.

But Gozo is more than just a haven for sun-seekers - it's also a treasure trove of history and culture, with a legacy that stretches back thousands of years. Explore the ancient citadel of Victoria, where narrow streets wind their way past medieval churches and noble palaces. Marvel at the neolithic temples of Ggantija, some of the oldest freestanding structures in the world, and ponder the mysteries of the past as you wander through their ancient halls.

Venture further inland, and you'll discover a landscape dotted with quaint villages and rolling countryside. From the charming streets of Xaghra to the rustic beauty of Gharb, Gozo's villages offer a glimpse into traditional Maltese life, where time seems to move at a slower pace. Stop by a local market to sample fresh produce and artisanal goods, or sip on a glass of local wine as you watch the world go by from a sun-drenched terrace.

And no visit to Gozo would be complete without sampling the island's culinary delights. From hearty stews and freshly-caught seafood to sweet pastries and creamy cheeses, Gozo's cuisine is as diverse as it is delicious. Be sure to indulge in a traditional ftira, a local delicacy made with freshly-baked bread and topped with a variety of mouth-watering ingredients.

So, whether you're seeking adventure in the great outdoors or craving a taste of authentic Maltese culture, Gozo has something to offer every traveller. Welcome to Gozo - where island escapades await around every corner, and the beauty of nature is always close at hand.

Comino: Blue Lagoon Bliss

Welcome to Comino, a tiny yet spectacular island nestled between the larger islands of Malta and Gozo. Known for its crystalline waters and breathtaking landscapes, Comino is a true haven for those seeking a slice of paradise in the heart of the Mediterranean.

As you approach Comino by boat, you'll be greeted by the sight of the island's most famous attraction - the Blue Lagoon. Renowned for its vibrant turquoise waters and pristine white sands, the Blue Lagoon is a postcard-perfect destination that draws visitors from far and wide. Dive into the cool, clear waters and snorkel amongst a kaleidoscope of marine life, or simply relax on the sun-drenched shores and soak up the natural beauty that surrounds you.

But Comino is more than just a beach destination - it's also a paradise for nature lovers and outdoor enthusiasts. Lace up your hiking boots and explore the island's rugged coastline, where hidden coves and secret caves await around every bend. Keep your eyes peeled for the native flora and fauna that call Comino home, from colourful wildflowers to majestic seabirds soaring overhead.

For those seeking a bit of adventure, Comino offers plenty of opportunities for exploration both above and below the surface. Kayak through hidden sea caves and rocky arches, or embark on a boat tour to discover the island's secluded bays and hidden coves. And if you're feeling particularly adventurous, why not try your hand at cliff jumping and experience the thrill of leaping into the azure waters below?

As the sun begins to dip below the horizon, settle in for a magical sunset over the Blue Lagoon, where the sky is ablaze with hues of pink, orange, and gold. Sip on a refreshing cocktail as you watch the last rays of light dance across the water, and feel the stresses of everyday life melt away in the tranquillity of this island paradise.

So, whether you're seeking relaxation on sun-drenched shores or adventure in the great outdoors, Comino offers a little slice of heaven for everyone to enjoy. Welcome to the Blue Lagoon Bliss of Comino - where the beauty of nature takes centre stage, and every moment is a memory in the making.

St. John's Co-Cathedral: Baroque Beauty

Welcome to St. John's Co-Cathedral, a dazzling jewel of Baroque architecture nestled in the heart of Valletta, Malta's capital city. As you step through the grand entrance of this magnificent cathedral, prepare to be transported back in time to an era of opulence, elegance, and spiritual splendour.

Built by the Knights of St. John between 1572 and 1577, St. John's Co-Cathedral stands as a testament to the wealth and power of the order, who sought to create a sanctuary worthy of their patron saint, St. John the Baptist. Designed by the renowned Maltese architect Girolamo Cassar, the cathedral is a masterpiece of Baroque design, with its ornate facade and intricate interior detailing leaving visitors in awe of its beauty.

As you step into the hallowed halls of St. John's, you'll be greeted by a symphony of colour and light that dances across the cathedral's intricately-decorated walls and ceilings. Marvel at the stunning frescoes and gilded stucco work that adorn the nave, each telling a story of faith, devotion, and divine inspiration.

But it's the cathedral's famed Caravaggio paintings that truly steal the show, with their masterful use of light and shadow bringing the biblical scenes to life in breathtaking detail. Stand before "The Beheading of St. John the Baptist" and "St. Jerome Writing," and feel the power and emotion radiating from these timeless masterpieces.

As you explore the cathedral further, don't forget to pay a visit to the Oratory of the Blessed Sacrament, where the exquisite marble tomb of Grand Master Jean de la Cassière lies in eternal repose. Admire the intricate carvings and delicate filigree work that adorn this sacred space, and take a moment to reflect on the lives of those who have come before.

Whether you're a history buff, an art enthusiast, or simply a traveller in search of beauty and inspiration, St. John's Co-Cathedral offers a feast for the senses that is sure to leave a lasting impression. Welcome to St. John's Co-Cathedral - where Baroque beauty meets spiritual serenity, and the legacy of Malta's past shines bright for all to see.

The Three Cities: Historic Havens

Welcome to the Three Cities, a trio of historic havens that have borne witness to centuries of conquest, intrigue, and cultural exchange. Situated on the eastern coast of Malta, facing the shimmering waters of the Grand Harbour, the Three Cities - Vittoriosa, Senglea, and Cospicua - stand as living testaments to the island's rich and diverse past.

Step back in time as you wander through the labyrinthine streets of Vittoriosa, the oldest of the Three Cities and a bastion of medieval fortifications. Marvel at the imposing walls of the Fort St. Angelo, where the Knights of St. John once stood guard over the island against invaders from across the Mediterranean. Lose yourself in the winding alleyways of the Collachio, the ancient heart of Vittoriosa, where centuries-old buildings and hidden courtyards await around every corner.

As you make your way across the Grand Harbour to Senglea, you'll be greeted by the sight of its majestic fortifications, which once served as the first line of defence for the island against enemy fleets. Explore the quaint streets and charming squares of this historic city, where the echoes of Malta's past mingle with the sounds of everyday life. Climb to the top of Gardjola Gardens for panoramic views of the harbour below, and imagine yourself standing watch over the bustling port as ships come and go on the horizon.

Finally, make your way to Cospicua, the largest of the Three Cities and a thriving hub of maritime activity since ancient times. Explore the bustling waterfront, where traditional fishing boats bob gently in the harbour and fishermen mend their nets in the shade of ancient warehouses. Wander through the narrow streets of the Collachio, where colourful balconies and ornate doorways add a touch of Mediterranean charm to the historic surroundings.

But the Three Cities are more than just relics of Malta's past - they're also vibrant communities where history and modernity intersect in perfect harmony. From lively festivals and cultural events to charming cafes and waterfront restaurants, there's always something happening in the Three Cities to captivate the imagination and inspire the soul.

So, whether you're a history buff, an architecture enthusiast, or simply a traveller in search of authentic Maltese charm, the Three Cities offer a treasure trove of experiences waiting to be discovered. Welcome to the Three Cities - where historic havens await around every corner, and the spirit of Malta's past lives on in every stone.

Marsaxlokk: Fishing Village Charm

Welcome to Marsaxlokk, a quaint fishing village nestled on the southeastern coast of Malta, where time seems to slow down amidst the tranquil waters of the Mediterranean. With its vibrant waterfront, colourful fishing boats, and laid-back atmosphere, Marsaxlokk exudes a charm that is as irresistible as it is authentic.

As you wander through the narrow streets of Marsaxlokk, you'll be greeted by the sight of traditional Maltese houses adorned with brightly-painted balconies and fragrant bougainvillaea. Follow your nose to the village's bustling fish market, where local fishermen gather each morning to sell their catch of the day, from fresh swordfish to succulent octopus. Watch as the morning sun dances across the water, casting a golden glow over the scene and infusing the air with the salty tang of the sea.

But Marsaxlokk is more than just a place to buy fish - it's also a hub of activity and culture, where traditions old and new come together in perfect harmony. Explore the village's charming cafes and restaurants, where you can savour delicious seafood dishes made with the freshest ingredients straight from the sea. Sample local delicacies like lampuki pie and fenkata, and wash it all down with a glass of crisp Maltese wine or a refreshing pint of local beer.

For a taste of Marsaxlokk's seafaring heritage, take a stroll along the waterfront and admire the village's iconic Luzzu boats, with their distinctive painted eyes that are said to ward off evil spirits and protect the fishermen at sea. Marvel at the craftsmanship and skill that goes into each boat's construction, and imagine yourself setting sail on the azure waters of the Mediterranean, following in the footsteps of generations of Maltese fishermen.

And if you're lucky enough to visit Marsaxlokk on a Sunday, be sure to check out the village's famous market, where local artisans and craftsmen sell everything from handmade lace to traditional Maltese pottery. Lose yourself in the bustling stalls and lively atmosphere, and pick up a unique souvenir to remind you of your time in this charming fishing village.

So, whether you're a foodie, a history buff, or simply a traveller in search of authentic Maltese charm, Marsaxlokk offers a little slice of heaven for everyone to enjoy. Welcome to Marsaxlokk - where fishing village charm meets Mediterranean magic, and every moment is a memory in the making.

Blue Grotto: Azure Wonders

Nestled along the rugged southern coast of Malta lies a natural wonder that captivates the imagination and enchants the senses - the Blue Grotto. This mesmerising sea cave complex is renowned for its dazzling azure waters and breathtaking rock formations, making it a must-visit destination for travellers seeking to explore the beauty of the Mediterranean.

As you approach the Blue Grotto by boat, you'll be greeted by the sight of towering limestone cliffs rising majestically from the sea, their rugged faces weathered by millennia of wind and waves. But it's what lies beneath the surface that truly sets the Blue Grotto apart - a labyrinth of sea caves and caverns that glow with an otherworldly blue light, casting an ethereal spell over all who venture inside.

Step aboard your boat and prepare to be whisked away on a journey through this underwater wonderland, where every twist and turn reveals a new marvel waiting to be discovered. Glide through narrow passages and into hidden chambers, where shafts of sunlight filter through the crystal-clear waters, illuminating the vibrant hues of the cave walls and sea floor below.

As you delve deeper into the Blue Grotto, you'll encounter a kaleidoscope of colours and textures that seem to dance and shimmer in the shifting light. Marvel at the delicate formations of stalactites and stalagmites that adorn the cave ceilings and floors, each one a testament to the power and beauty of nature's handiwork.

But perhaps the most magical moment of all comes when you reach the heart of the Blue Grotto, where the sunlight reflects off the water in a dazzling display of blues and greens that seem to defy description. It's a sight that will stay with you long after you've left the cave behind, a memory to cherish and treasure for years to come.

So, whether you're a nature lover, an adventure seeker, or simply someone who appreciates the beauty of the natural world, the Blue Grotto offers an experience like no other. Prepare to be spellbound by the azure wonders that await you in this breathtaking sea cave complex, and let the beauty of the Mediterranean wash over you like a gentle tide.

Hypogeum: Ancient Mysteries

Hidden beneath the bustling streets of Paola, on the island of Malta, lies a place shrouded in mystery and intrigue - the Hypogeum. This subterranean marvel is one of the world's most remarkable archaeological sites, offering a rare glimpse into the lives and rituals of Malta's ancient inhabitants.

Dating back over 5,000 years, the Hypogeum is believed to have been originally carved out of solid limestone by the prehistoric inhabitants of Malta, known as the Temple Builders. Over the centuries, it served as a place of worship, burial, and ritual, with its labyrinthine chambers and passageways holding untold secrets waiting to be uncovered.

As you descend into the depths of the Hypogeum, you'll be struck by the sheer scale and complexity of this ancient underground complex. Marvel at the intricately-carved chambers and halls, where the walls are adorned with mysterious symbols and motifs that hint at the spiritual beliefs and practices of Malta's ancient inhabitants.

But it's the Hypogeum's famous Oracle Room that truly captures the imagination. Carved out of solid rock and known for its remarkable acoustic properties, this chamber is believed to have been used for sacred rituals and ceremonies, where priests would commune with the spirits of the ancestors and divine the future through the power of sound.

As you explore further into the depths of the Hypogeum, you'll encounter a series of burial chambers and ossuaries, where the remains of thousands of individuals lie interred, their ancient bones bearing silent witness to the passage of time. It's a sobering reminder of the fragility of life and the enduring power of the human spirit.

But the Hypogeum is more than just a monument to the past - it's also a living testament to Malta's rich cultural heritage and the enduring legacy of its ancient inhabitants. As you emerge back into the light of day, you'll carry with you a sense of wonder and awe at the mysteries that lie hidden beneath the surface of this remarkable island.

Prepare to be transported back in time to a world of ancient wonders and enigmatic rituals as you explore the depths of the Hypogeum, and let the echoes of Malta's past guide you on a journey of discovery unlike any other.

Golden Bay: Sun-soaked Serenity

Nestled along the northwest coast of Malta lies a hidden gem that beckons travellers seeking solace amidst the beauty of the Mediterranean - Golden Bay. This idyllic stretch of coastline is renowned for its golden sands, azure waters, and breathtaking sunsets, making it a favourite destination for locals and visitors alike.

As you make your way to Golden Bay, you'll be struck by the sheer beauty of the landscape that unfolds before you. Rolling hills dotted with wildflowers give way to rugged cliffs that plunge dramatically into the sea, creating a dramatic backdrop for the pristine beach that lies below.

Step onto the soft, powdery sands of Golden Bay and feel the warmth of the sun on your skin as you gaze out over the crystal-clear waters of the Mediterranean. Dip your toes into the cool, refreshing sea and feel the stresses of everyday life melt away in the gentle embrace of the waves.

But Golden Bay is more than just a place to soak up the sun - it's also a paradise for outdoor enthusiasts and adventure seekers. Take a leisurely stroll along the water's edge and explore the hidden coves and rocky outcrops that line the coastline, or venture out into the open sea on a thrilling boat tour or snorkelling excursion.

For those seeking a bit of tranquillity, find a quiet spot on the beach and bask in the serenity of your surroundings as you watch the world go by. Listen to the gentle lapping of the waves against the shore and feel the gentle sea breeze caress your skin as you lose yourself in the beauty of nature.

And as the day draws to a close, prepare to be dazzled by one of Golden Bay's most breathtaking sights - the sunset. Watch in awe as the sky is painted in hues of pink, orange, and gold, casting a warm glow over the horizon and illuminating the sea in a shimmering cascade of light.

Whether you're seeking relaxation, adventure, or simply a moment of peace and quiet, Golden Bay offers a little slice of paradise for everyone to enjoy. So pack your sunscreen, grab your towel, and prepare to experience the sun-soaked serenity of Golden Bay for yourself.

Dingli Cliffs: Majestic Heights

Perched on the western coast of Malta, overlooking the shimmering expanse of the Mediterranean Sea, the Dingli Cliffs stand as a testament to the island's rugged beauty and natural splendour. Rising majestically from the sea to heights of over 250 metres, these imposing limestone cliffs offer visitors a breathtaking panorama of the surrounding landscape and a sense of awe-inspiring grandeur.

As you approach the Dingli Cliffs, you'll feel a sense of anticipation building within you, knowing that you're about to witness one of Malta's most iconic natural wonders. The cliffs stretch for several kilometres along the coastline, their sheer faces carved by the relentless forces of wind and water over millennia. Yet despite their imposing stature, there's an undeniable sense of tranquillity that pervades the air, making the Dingli Cliffs a haven for those seeking solitude and contemplation amidst the beauty of nature.

Step to the edge of the cliffs and gaze out over the vast expanse of the Mediterranean Sea, where the horizon stretches endlessly into the distance, punctuated only by the occasional sailboat or seabird gliding on the breeze. Feel the cool sea breeze on your face and listen to the sound of waves crashing against the rocky shore far below, a symphony of nature's own making that soothes the soul and invigorates the spirit.

But the Dingli Cliffs are more than just a scenic viewpoint - they're also steeped in history and cultural significance. Take a leisurely stroll along the cliff-top path and discover ancient cart ruts carved into the limestone, a testament to Malta's prehistoric past. Visit the nearby Chapel of St. Mary Magdalene, where locals and visitors alike come to seek solace and offer prayers amidst the tranquillity of the cliffs.

As the sun begins to dip below the horizon, prepare to witness one of nature's most spectacular displays - the sunset. Watch in awe as the sky is set ablaze with hues of red, orange, and gold, casting a warm glow over the cliffs and illuminating the sea in a breathtaking cascade of light. It's a sight that will stay with you long after you've left the cliffs behind, a memory to cherish and treasure for years to come.

So whether you're a nature lover, a history enthusiast, or simply someone in search of a moment of quiet contemplation, the Dingli Cliffs offer a truly majestic experience that is sure to leave a lasting impression. Prepare to be swept away by the beauty and grandeur of Malta's tallest cliffs, and let the majesty of the Dingli Cliffs take your breath away.

Mellieha: Sandy Shores

Nestled on the northern coast of Malta, Mellieha beckons with its sandy shores and laid-back atmosphere, offering travellers a tranquil escape from the hustle and bustle of everyday life. As you approach this charming seaside town, you'll be struck by its picturesque setting, with the sparkling waters of the Mediterranean stretching out before you and the towering cliffs of the nearby countryside framing the horizon.

Mellieha is perhaps best known for its stunning beaches, which rank among the finest on the island. Golden Bay, one of Malta's most popular beaches, offers pristine sands and crystal-clear waters perfect for swimming, sunbathing, and water sports. Nearby Ghajn Tuffieha Bay boasts a more secluded vibe, with its rugged cliffs and lush vegetation providing a dramatic backdrop to the azure sea.

But Mellieha is more than just a beach destination - it's also steeped in history and culture, with plenty of attractions to explore. Visit the imposing Sanctuary of Our Lady of Mellieha, a beautiful church perched on a hill overlooking the town, and marvel at its intricate architecture and stunning views. Explore the ancient catacombs of St. Agatha's Chapel, where you can glimpse Malta's early Christian heritage up close.

For those seeking adventure, Mellieha offers plenty of opportunities to explore the great outdoors. Lace up your hiking boots and trek through the scenic countryside surrounding the town, where you'll discover hidden valleys, rugged cliffs, and panoramic vistas that will take your breath away. Or, take to the water and embark on a boat tour of the nearby islands, where you can snorkel, dive, and explore hidden coves and sea caves.

After a day of adventure and exploration, unwind with a leisurely stroll through Mellieha's charming streets, where you'll find quaint cafes, family-run restaurants, and bustling markets selling local produce and handicrafts. Sample traditional Maltese delicacies like rabbit stew and pastizzi, and wash it all down with a glass of locally-produced wine or a refreshing pint of local beer.

Whether you're seeking relaxation on sun-drenched shores, adventure in the great outdoors, or a taste of Malta's rich history and culture, Mellieha offers something for everyone to enjoy. So pack your bags, grab your sunscreen, and prepare to experience the sandy shores of Mellieha for yourself.

Tarxien Temples: Prehistoric Marvels

Nestled in the heart of Malta lies a remarkable archaeological site that offers a glimpse into the island's ancient past - the Tarxien Temples. Dating back over 5,000 years, these megalithic structures are among the oldest freestanding buildings in the world, making them a must-visit destination for history buffs and curious travellers alike.

As you approach the Tarxien Temples, you'll be struck by the sheer scale and complexity of these ancient marvels. Comprising four separate structures built from massive limestone blocks, the temples are thought to have been constructed between 3600 and 2500 BC by Malta's prehistoric inhabitants, known as the Temple Builders. Each temple is adorned with intricate carvings and sculptures depicting animals, plants, and human figures, offering tantalising clues about the spiritual beliefs and cultural practices of Malta's ancient civilisation.

Step inside the temples and marvel at the ingenuity and skill of the Temple Builders, who managed to quarry, transport, and assemble these massive stone blocks without the aid of modern tools or machinery. Wander through the labyrinthine chambers and passageways, where shafts of sunlight filter through the roof openings, casting a soft glow over the ancient stone walls and floors.

But it's the temple's ornate carvings and decorations that truly steal the show. Admire the intricate patterns and motifs that adorn the walls and altars, each one a testament to the craftsmanship and artistic skill of Malta's ancient artisans. Marvel at the lifelike depictions of animals and humans, and ponder the meaning behind these ancient symbols and scenes.

As you explore further, you'll discover a series of mysterious chambers and recesses, some of which are thought to have been used for rituals and ceremonies. Imagine the sound of chanting voices and the flickering light of torches as priests and worshippers gathered to honour their gods and ancestors, and feel a sense of reverence for the ancient rituals that took place within these sacred walls.

Today, the Tarxien Temples stand as a reminder of Malta's rich cultural heritage and the enduring legacy of its ancient inhabitants. Whether you're a history enthusiast, an archaeology buff, or simply someone with a curiosity for the past, a visit to the Tarxien Temples is sure to leave you awestruck by the ingenuity and creativity of Malta's prehistoric people.

Sliema: Coastal Chic

Along the northeastern coast of Malta lies the vibrant seaside town of Sliema, a destination that effortlessly blends coastal charm with modern sophistication. As you approach Sliema, you'll be greeted by a bustling promenade lined with palm trees, chic cafes, and stylish boutiques, where locals and visitors alike come to see and be seen.

Sliema's coastal location has long made it a popular destination for those seeking sun, sea, and relaxation. With its rocky beaches and clear blue waters, it's the perfect spot to soak up the Mediterranean sunshine and enjoy a refreshing dip in the sea. Whether you're lounging on the beach with a good book or indulging in water sports like snorkelling or kayaking, Sliema offers plenty of opportunities to enjoy the great outdoors.

But Sliema is more than just a beach destination - it's also a hub of culture, entertainment, and nightlife. Take a leisurely stroll along the waterfront and admire the stunning views of Valletta's historic skyline across the harbour, or explore the town's charming streets and alleyways, where you'll find hidden gems like art galleries, theatres, and live music venues.

For those with a passion for shopping, Sliema is a true paradise. From designer boutiques and high-end fashion stores to quirky markets and artisanal shops, there's something for every taste and budget. Treat yourself to a new wardrobe, pick up a unique souvenir to remind you of your trip, or simply spend the day browsing and people-watching along the bustling streets of Sliema.

And when it comes to dining, Sliema certainly doesn't disappoint. With its wide range of restaurants, cafes, and eateries, you'll find everything from traditional Maltese cuisine to international favourites and gourmet delights. Whether you're craving fresh seafood, authentic Italian pizza, or a hearty British pub meal, you'll find it all in Sliema.

As the sun sets and the stars come out, Sliema truly comes alive with an array of nightlife options to suit every taste. Enjoy a leisurely cocktail on a rooftop terrace overlooking the harbour, dance the night away at a trendy nightclub, or simply unwind with a quiet drink in a cosy wine bar. Whatever your preference, Sliema offers endless opportunities for fun and relaxation after dark.

So whether you're seeking sun-soaked relaxation, coastal chic, or vibrant nightlife, Sliema has it all and more. With its stunning seaside setting, rich cultural heritage, and lively atmosphere, it's no wonder that Sliema remains one of Malta's most beloved destinations for travellers from around the world.

Hagar Qim and Mnajdra Temples: Megalithic Marvels

Nestled amidst the rugged landscape of Malta's southwestern coast lie two of the island's most extraordinary archaeological sites - the Hagar Qim and Mnajdra Temples. Dating back over 5,000 years, these megalithic marvels are among the oldest religious structures in the world and offer a fascinating glimpse into Malta's prehistoric past.

As you approach the Hagar Qim and Mnajdra Temples, you'll be struck by the sheer scale and grandeur of these ancient monuments. Built from massive limestone blocks and surrounded by sweeping vistas of the Mediterranean Sea, the temples are a testament to the ingenuity and craftsmanship of Malta's ancient inhabitants, known as the Temple Builders.

Step inside the temples and marvel at the intricate carvings and sculptures that adorn the walls and altars, each one a testament to the spiritual beliefs and cultural practices of Malta's prehistoric people. Admire the precision with which the massive stone blocks were quarried, transported, and assembled, and ponder the significance of the temples' alignment with the movements of the sun and stars. But it's not just the temples themselves that are impressive - it's also their stunning natural setting. Perched atop cliffs overlooking the sea, the Hagar Qim and Mnajdra Temples offer panoramic views of Malta's rugged coastline and crystal-clear waters, providing the perfect backdrop for a day of exploration and discovery.

As you wander through the temples and explore their ancient chambers and passageways, you'll discover a wealth of archaeological treasures, from intricate pottery fragments to delicate figurines and ceremonial objects. Each artefact offers tantalising clues about the lives and rituals of Malta's ancient inhabitants, shedding light on a lost world that continues to captivate the imagination of archaeologists and historians to this day.

But perhaps the most remarkable aspect of the Hagar Qim and Mnajdra Temples is their enduring mystery. Despite decades of study and excavation, much about these ancient sites remains unknown, leaving plenty of room for speculation and debate. From the purpose of the temples to the identity of their builders, the Hagar Qim and Mnajdra Temples continue to intrigue and inspire visitors from around the world, inviting them to embark on a journey of discovery through Malta's ancient past.

So whether you're a history enthusiast, an archaeology buff, or simply someone with a curiosity for the mysteries of the past, a visit to the Hagar Qim and Mnajdra Temples is sure to leave you awe-struck by the megalithic marvels of Malta's prehistoric heritage.

Rabat: Historical Enclave

Nestled in the heart of Malta, just a stone's throw away from the ancient city of Mdina, lies the historic enclave of Rabat. With its winding streets, centuries-old buildings, and rich cultural heritage, Rabat offers visitors a glimpse into Malta's storied past and a chance to step back in time to a bygone era.

As you wander through Rabat's charming streets, you'll be struck by the sense of history that pervades the air. From the imposing walls of the medieval town to the quaint squares and hidden courtyards tucked away around every corner, Rabat is a living museum of Maltese heritage, where the past seamlessly blends with the present.

One of Rabat's most iconic landmarks is the Catacombs of St. Paul and St. Agatha, a sprawling underground complex that once served as a burial site for Malta's early Christians. Explore the labyrinthine passages and chambers of these ancient catacombs, where the remains of thousands of individuals lie interred, their ancient tombs adorned with intricate carvings and decorations.

But Rabat's historical treasures aren't confined to underground chambers - they're also on full display in the town's many churches and museums. Visit the impressive St. Paul's Church, built atop the site where the apostle is said to have taken refuge during his time in Malta, and admire its stunning Baroque architecture and ornate interior. Or, step inside the Wignacourt Museum and discover a treasure trove of Maltese art, artefacts, and archaeological finds spanning thousands of years of history.

For those with a passion for history and archaeology, Rabat offers plenty of opportunities for exploration and discovery. Visit the Domus Romana, a beautifully-preserved Roman townhouse dating back to the 1st century BC, and marvel at its intricate mosaics, frescoes, and ancient artifacts. Or, take a leisurely stroll through the gardens of the Casa Bernard, a historic palazzo that offers stunning views of Rabat and the surrounding countryside.

As the sun begins to set and the shadows lengthen, Rabat takes on a magical air, with the soft glow of streetlights casting a warm light over the ancient streets and buildings. Grab a seat at one of the town's charming cafes or restaurants and savour a delicious meal of traditional Maltese cuisine, or simply wander the streets and soak up the atmosphere as the town comes alive with the sounds of laughter and conversation.

Whether you're a history enthusiast, a culture vulture, or simply a traveller in search of authentic Maltese charm, Rabat offers a wealth of experiences waiting to be discovered. So pack your bags, lace up your walking shoes, and prepare to embark on a journey through the historical enclave of Rabat - where every corner holds a story waiting to be told.

Fort St. Elmo: Military Heritage

Perched proudly at the tip of the Sciberras Peninsula in Valletta, Fort St. Elmo stands as a testament to Malta's rich military heritage and strategic importance throughout history. This formidable fortress has witnessed centuries of conflict and conquest, serving as a key stronghold for the Knights of St. John, the British Empire, and Malta's own armed forces.

As you approach Fort St. Elmo, you'll be struck by its imposing walls and commanding position overlooking the entrance to the Grand Harbour. Built in the late 16th century by the Knights of St. John, the fortress was originally intended to defend Malta against invasion by the Ottoman Empire, and its sturdy construction and strategic location made it an impregnable bastion of defence.

Step inside the walls of Fort St. Elmo and you'll find yourself transported back in time to a world of military intrigue and strategic manoeuvring. Explore the fortress's labyrinthine passages, barracks, and gun emplacements, where you can still see the scars of battles fought and won centuries ago. Marvel at the stunning views of the Grand Harbour and the surrounding cityscape from the fortress's ramparts, and imagine the awe-inspiring sight of hundreds of ships sailing into battle on the horizon.

But Fort St. Elmo is more than just a relic of Malta's martial past - it's also a living museum that offers visitors a chance to delve into the island's rich military history. Visit the National War Museum, housed within the fortress's walls, and discover a treasure trove of artefacts, memorabilia, and interactive exhibits that tell the story of Malta's role in some of the most pivotal conflicts of the past few centuries. From the Great Siege of 1565 to World War II and beyond, the museum offers a fascinating insight into Malta's enduring spirit of resilience and courage in the face of adversity.

For those with a passion for military history and architecture, Fort St. Elmo is a must-visit destination that promises to captivate and inspire. Whether you're a history buff, an avid photographer, or simply someone with a curiosity for the past, a visit to this iconic fortress is sure to leave a lasting impression and a newfound appreciation for Malta's storied military heritage. So lace up your boots, grab your camera, and prepare to embark on a journey through the annals of time at Fort St. Elmo - where the echoes of history still ring loud and clear.

The Malta Experience: History Unveiled

Imagine stepping into a time machine, whisking you away to a land where ancient civilizations clashed, knights defended their honour, and empires rose and fell. Welcome to "The Malta Experience," an immersive journey through the rich tapestry of Malta's history, where the past comes to life in vivid detail and captivating storytelling.

Situated in the heart of Valletta, Malta's capital city and a UNESCO World Heritage Site, "The Malta Experience" is more than just a museum - it's an adventure through time that promises to enlighten, educate, and entertain visitors of all ages. From the moment you step through the doors, you'll be transported back in time to the earliest days of Malta's history, where Neolithic settlers carved out a life on these rocky shores over 7,000 years ago.

As you make your way through the exhibits, you'll encounter the ancient civilizations that shaped Malta's destiny, from the Phoenicians and Romans to the Arabs and Normans. Marvel at the intricate pottery, tools, and artefacts left behind by these early inhabitants, and gain a newfound appreciation for their ingenuity and resourcefulness in the face of adversity. But it's not just ancient history on display at "The Malta

Experience" - the museum also offers a fascinating insight into Malta's more recent past, including its pivotal role in World War II and its journey to independence in the 20th century. Discover the stories of courage, sacrifice, and resilience that defined Malta's wartime experience, and learn how the island's strategic location made it a key battleground in the fight for freedom and democracy. One of the highlights of "The Malta Experience" is its state-of-the-art audiovisual presentation, which brings Malta's history to life in stunning detail. Sit back and immerse yourself in the sights and sounds of Malta's past, from the epic battles of the Great Siege to the triumphs and tragedies of modern times. Through the magic of technology, you'll feel as if you've been transported back in time to witness these historic events firsthand, gaining a deeper understanding of Malta's place in the world and its enduring spirit of resilience.

As you emerge from "The Malta Experience," you'll carry with you a newfound appreciation for the rich tapestry of history that has shaped this remarkable island nation. From its humble beginnings as a Neolithic settlement to its emergence as a modern European state, Malta's journey is a testament to the resilience of its people and the enduring power of its cultural heritage. So come and discover the history of Malta as you've never seen it before at "The Malta Experience" - where every exhibit tells a story and every moment is a chance to learn and grow.

Popeye Village: Fun for All Ages

Tucked away on the scenic coast of Anchor Bay in the quaint village of Mellieħa, lies a place where childhood dreams come to life and fun knows no bounds - Popeye Village. This charming attraction, originally built as a film set for the 1980 musical production of "Popeye," has since evolved into a beloved theme park that delights visitors of all ages with its whimsical charm and nostalgic appeal.

As you approach Popeye Village, you'll be greeted by a colourful array of wooden buildings perched on the rocky shoreline, overlooking the sparkling waters of the Mediterranean Sea. The village itself is a sight to behold, with its quaint streets, bustling market stalls, and charming cafes evoking the spirit of a bygone era.

Step inside Popeye Village and prepare to be transported to the fictional town of Sweethaven, where the beloved cartoon character Popeye and his friends come to life in a series of interactive attractions and live shows. Join Popeye, Olive Oyl, and the rest of the gang as they embark on a series of misadventures and escapades, from daring rescue missions to comedic mishaps, all set against the backdrop of this whimsical seaside village.

For the young and the young at heart, Popeye Village offers a wealth of activities and entertainment to enjoy. Climb aboard the vintage-style sailboats and take a leisurely cruise around Anchor Bay, or splash around in the village's very own waterpark, complete with slides, splash pools, and water cannons galore. Explore the village's many themed play areas, from the Pirate's Cove to the Spinach Factory, where you can test your strength and agility in a series of fun-filled challenges.

But Popeye Village isn't just about rides and attractions - it's also a place where you can relax and unwind amidst the beauty of Malta's natural landscape. Take a leisurely stroll along the village's scenic boardwalks and admire the stunning views of Anchor Bay and the surrounding countryside, or enjoy a picnic on the village green as you soak up the sunshine and sea breeze.

As the day draws to a close, be sure to catch one of Popeye Village's famous live shows, where talented performers bring the beloved characters of Popeye and his friends to life in a series of hilarious and heartwarming performances. From high-flying acrobatics to toe-tapping musical numbers, these shows are sure to leave you laughing, cheering, and wanting more.

Whether you're a fan of the classic cartoon or simply someone in search of a fun-filled day out, Popeye Village offers something for everyone to enjoy. So pack your sense of adventure, grab your family and friends, and prepare to embark on a journey of laughter, excitement, and fun at Popeye Village - where the spirit of Sweethaven lives on in all its whimsical glory.

Marsaskala: Tranquil Seaside Retreat

Perched on the southeastern coast of Malta, overlooking the shimmering waters of the Mediterranean Sea, lies the charming seaside town of Marsaskala. With its picturesque harbour, sandy beaches, and laid-back atmosphere, Marsaskala is the perfect destination for travellers seeking a tranquil retreat away from the hustle and bustle of city life.

As you arrive in Marsaskala, you'll be struck by the town's idyllic setting, with its colourful fishing boats bobbing in the harbour and the scent of saltwater in the air. Nestled between rugged cliffs and rolling countryside, Marsaskala offers visitors a chance to reconnect with nature and enjoy the simple pleasures of coastal living.

One of the highlights of Marsaskala is its stunning coastline, which boasts several sandy beaches and secluded coves perfect for sunbathing, swimming, and snorkelling. Whether you prefer to relax on the soft sands of St. Thomas Bay or explore the crystal-clear waters of Zonqor Point, there's plenty of opportunity to soak up the sun and enjoy the refreshing sea breeze.

But Marsaskala is more than just a beach destination - it's also a haven for food lovers, with a wide range of restaurants, cafes, and eateries serving up delicious Maltese and Mediterranean cuisine. From fresh seafood caught straight from the sea to hearty pasta dishes and mouth-watering desserts, there's something to satisfy every palate in Marsaskala.

For those interested in history and culture, Marsaskala offers plenty of opportunities for exploration and discovery. Visit the nearby St. Thomas Tower, a 16th-century coastal fortification built by the Knights of St. John to defend Malta against invasion, and marvel at its impressive architecture and stunning views of the surrounding coastline. Or, take a leisurely stroll through the town's charming streets and squares, where you'll find quaint churches, historic buildings, and traditional Maltese architecture at every turn.

As the sun sets and the stars come out, Marsaskala takes on a magical air, with its waterfront promenade coming alive with the sound of laughter and conversation. Grab a seat at one of the town's many cafes or bars and enjoy a leisurely drink as you watch the world go by, or simply take a quiet evening stroll along the harbour and admire the twinkling lights of the fishing boats reflected in the water.

Whether you're seeking relaxation, adventure, or simply a chance to unwind in a beautiful seaside setting, Marsaskala has something for everyone to enjoy. So pack your bags, leave your worries behind, and prepare to experience the tranquil charm of Malta's coastal gem - Marsaskala.

Mosta Dome: Architectural Wonder

Standing proudly in the heart of the quaint town of Mosta, the Mosta Dome, also known as the Rotunda of Mosta, is a true architectural marvel that has captured the hearts and imaginations of visitors for centuries. This iconic landmark, with its majestic dome towering over the surrounding landscape, is not only a testament to the skill and ingenuity of its builders but also a symbol of resilience and faith that has endured the test of time.

As you approach the Mosta Dome, you can't help but be awestruck by its sheer size and grandeur. The exterior, with its neoclassical façade and towering Corinthian columns, exudes an air of timeless elegance, while the massive dome, one of the largest in Europe, dominates the skyline and draws your gaze upwards in wonder.

Step inside the Mosta Dome, and you'll find yourself transported to a world of beauty and serenity. The interior of the church is a masterpiece of Baroque architecture, with its soaring arches, ornate altars, and intricate frescoes that adorn every surface. Sunlight streams in through the stained glass windows, casting a soft, ethereal glow over the sacred space and filling it with a sense of peace and tranquillity.

But perhaps the most remarkable feature of the Mosta Dome is its incredible dome, which spans an impressive 37.2 metres in diameter and rises to a height of 61 metres above the ground. Constructed entirely without the use of scaffolding, the dome is a marvel of engineering and craftsmanship, a testament to the skill and dedication of its builders.

One of the most fascinating aspects of the Mosta Dome is its rich history and the role it played in Malta's wartime experience. During World War II, the church miraculously survived a direct hit from a German bomb that crashed through the dome during a mass, only to fail to detonate and harm a single soul. Today, the spot where the bomb landed is marked by a replica of the bomb itself, serving as a poignant reminder of the church's miraculous escape from destruction.

As you explore the Mosta Dome and learn about its fascinating history and architectural significance, you can't help but be struck by the sense of awe and reverence that fills the air. Whether you're a history buff, an architecture enthusiast, or simply someone in search of spiritual inspiration, a visit to the Mosta Dome is sure to leave a lasting impression and a newfound appreciation for Malta's rich cultural heritage. So come and discover the architectural wonder of the Mosta Dome - where history, beauty, and faith converge in perfect harmony.

Ta' Qali Crafts Village: Artisanal Treasures

Nestled amidst the picturesque countryside of central Malta lies a hidden gem for lovers of art, craft, and tradition - the Ta' Qali Crafts Village. Tucked away in the idyllic surroundings of Ta' Qali National Park, this charming village is a haven for artisans, craftsmen, and visitors seeking to discover the rich heritage and creative spirit of the Maltese people.

As you approach the Ta' Qali Crafts Village, you'll be greeted by a quaint cluster of stone buildings, each housing a unique array of workshops, studios, and boutiques showcasing the talents of Malta's finest artisans. From pottery and glassblowing to woodcarving and lace-making, there's no shortage of artisanal treasures waiting to be discovered within the village's winding streets and alleyways.

Step inside one of the workshops, and you'll find yourself immersed in a world of creativity and craftsmanship, where skilled artisans ply their trade using time-honoured techniques passed down through generations. Watch as master glassblowers transform molten glass into delicate works of art, or marvel at the precision and skill of a woodcarver as they carve intricate patterns and designs into fine timber.

But the Ta' Qali Crafts Village is more than just a place to admire beautiful objects - it's also a chance to get hands-on and try your hand at traditional crafts yourself. Many of the workshops offer interactive demonstrations and workshops where visitors can learn the basics of pottery, painting, or jewellery-making under the guidance of experienced artisans. Whether you're a novice or an experienced crafter, there's something for everyone to enjoy and explore within the village's creative community.

In addition to its workshops and studios, the Ta' Qali Crafts Village is also home to a vibrant market where visitors can browse and shop for a wide range of locally-made crafts, souvenirs, and gifts. From handmade ceramics and textiles to intricate jewellery and one-of-a-kind artworks, there's no shortage of unique treasures to be found among the market stalls and boutiques.

But perhaps the most rewarding part of a visit to the Ta' Qali Crafts Village is the opportunity to meet and connect with the talented artisans who call this place home. Strike up a conversation with a potter, weaver, or silversmith, and you'll discover not only their passion for their craft but also their deep connection to Malta's cultural heritage and traditions.

Whether you're a collector, a crafter, or simply someone with a love for beautiful things, a visit to the Ta' Qali Crafts Village is sure to inspire, delight, and captivate. So come and explore this hidden gem in the heart of Malta's countryside, and discover the artisanal treasures that await within the Ta' Qali Crafts Village.

Ghar Dalam Cave: Geological Wonders

Nestled on the southern coast of Malta, amidst the rugged limestone landscape of the Wied Babu valley, lies a natural wonder that has fascinated explorers and scientists for centuries - the Ghar Dalam Cave. This ancient cavern, whose name translates to "Cave of Darkness," offers visitors a unique opportunity to journey deep into the island's geological past and discover the secrets hidden within its rocky depths.

As you approach the entrance to Ghar Dalam Cave, you'll be struck by the sheer size and scale of this natural wonder. Carved out over millions of years by the relentless forces of wind and water, the cave extends deep into the earth, its dark and mysterious interior beckoning visitors to explore its hidden chambers and passageways.

Step inside the cave, and you'll find yourself transported back in time to a world long gone, where Malta was a very different place than it is today. The walls of Ghar Dalam Cave are lined with layers of sediment and rock, each one a testament to the island's ever-changing landscape and the ancient forces that shaped it.

But it's not just the geological formations that make Ghar Dalam Cave so special - it's also the wealth of archaeological treasures that have been unearthed within its depths. The cave is home to a vast collection of fossils, dating back over 500,000 years, that offer a fascinating glimpse into Malta's prehistoric past.

Among the most remarkable discoveries found within Ghar Dalam Cave are the remains of dwarf elephants and hippopotamuses, which once roamed the island during the Pleistocene era. These ancient creatures, along with a wide variety of other animal species, have been preserved in the cave's sedimentary layers, providing valuable insights into Malta's biodiversity and evolution over time.

As you explore the cave's interior, you'll also encounter evidence of human habitation dating back to the Neolithic period, including pottery shards, tools, and other artefacts left behind by Malta's earliest inhabitants. These archaeological finds offer a tantalising glimpse into the lives of Malta's ancient peoples and the ways in which they adapted to their harsh and unforgiving environment.

But perhaps the most striking aspect of Ghar Dalam Cave is its sheer beauty and sense of mystery. As you venture deeper into its depths, you'll be surrounded by the eerie silence and darkness of the underground world, punctuated only by the occasional drip of water and the echo of your footsteps on the rocky floor.

Whether you're a geology enthusiast, an archaeology buff, or simply someone with a sense of curiosity and adventure, a visit to Ghar Dalam Cave is sure to leave a lasting impression. So come and embark on a journey through Malta's geological wonders, and discover the secrets that lie hidden within the ancient depths of Ghar Dalam Cave.

Hal Saflieni Hypogeum: Subterranean Splendor

Nestled beneath the sun-soaked streets of Paola, on the southern coast of Malta, lies a subterranean wonder that has captured the imagination of archaeologists and historians for generations - the Hal Saflieni Hypogeum. This extraordinary underground complex, carved out of solid limestone over 5,000 years ago, offers visitors a glimpse into the mysterious world of Malta's prehistoric past and the ingenuity of its ancient inhabitants.

As you descend into the depths of the Hal Saflieni Hypogeum, you'll be struck by the sheer scale and sophistication of this remarkable underground structure. Spread out over three levels and spanning an area of over 500 square meters, the hypogeum is a labyrinth of passageways, chambers, and halls, all hewn from the living rock with astonishing precision and care.

Step inside the hypogeum, and you'll find yourself surrounded by a sense of awe and wonder as you explore its hidden treasures. Marvel at the intricate carvings and decorations that adorn the walls and ceilings of the chambers, depicting scenes of daily life, religious rituals, and mythical creatures that offer tantalising clues to the beliefs and customs of Malta's ancient peoples.

But perhaps the most remarkable feature of the Hal Saflieni Hypogeum is its acoustics, which have earned it the nickname "the Oracle Chamber." Step into this eerie chamber, and you'll be amazed to discover that even the faintest whisper can be heard clearly throughout the entire space, thanks to the unique properties of the limestone rock. It's believed that the chamber was used for ritualistic purposes, with sound playing a central role in ancient ceremonies and religious practices.

As you explore the hypogeum, you'll also encounter evidence of its use as a burial site, with the remains of over 7,000 individuals discovered within its chambers. These ancient tombs, some dating back over 5,000 years, offer a poignant reminder of the passage of time and the enduring mystery of Malta's prehistoric past.

But perhaps the most remarkable aspect of the Hal Saflieni Hypogeum is its sheer beauty and sense of mystery. As you wander through its dimly-lit corridors and chambers, you'll be enveloped by a sense of timelessness and wonder, as if you've stepped back in time to a world long forgotten.

Whether you're a history enthusiast, an archaeology buff, or simply someone with a sense of curiosity and adventure, a visit to the Hal Saflieni Hypogeum is sure to leave a lasting impression. So come and embark on a journey through Malta's subterranean splendor, and discover the secrets that lie hidden within the ancient depths of the Hal Saflieni Hypogeum.

Vittoriosa: Fortified Grandeur

Nestled on the southeastern shore of Malta's Grand Harbour, Vittoriosa stands as a testament to the island's rich maritime history and strategic importance throughout the ages. This historic city, also known as Birgu, is a treasure trove of architectural wonders, fortified walls, and centuries-old charm, offering visitors a glimpse into Malta's storied past and the legacy of its medieval knights.

As you approach Vittoriosa, you'll be greeted by its imposing fortifications, which have stood guard over the city for centuries, protecting it from invaders and would-be conquerors. Built by the Knights of St. John in the 16th century, these formidable walls are a testament to the military prowess and engineering skill of their creators, and offer a glimpse into the city's turbulent past.

Step inside the walls of Vittoriosa, and you'll find yourself transported back in time to a world of cobbled streets, ancient churches, and grand palaces, where the echoes of history linger around every corner. Wander through the city's labyrinthine alleys and squares, and you'll encounter a wealth of architectural treasures, from the grand Auberge de France to the ornate St. Lawrence's Church, each one a testament to Malta's rich cultural heritage.

But perhaps the most iconic landmark in Vittoriosa is the Fort St. Angelo, a mighty fortress that has played a central role in Malta's history for over a thousand years. Originally built by the Arabs in the 9th century, the fortress was later strengthened and expanded by the Knights of St. John, who made it their headquarters during their rule of Malta. Today, Fort St. Angelo stands as a symbol of Malta's resilience and determination in the face of adversity, and offers visitors a chance to explore its ancient ramparts and soak in the breathtaking views of the Grand Harbour below.

In addition to its historic landmarks, Vittoriosa is also home to a vibrant community of artisans, craftsmen, and traders, who ply their trade in the city's bustling markets and workshops. From handcrafted jewellery and pottery to traditional Maltese delicacies, there's no shortage of treasures to be found among the city's narrow streets and hidden alleyways.

Whether you're a history buff, an architecture enthusiast, or simply someone in search of adventure and exploration, a visit to Vittoriosa promises to be an unforgettable experience. So come and immerse yourself in the fortified grandeur of Malta's ancient city, and discover the rich tapestry of history and culture that awaits within the walls of Vittoriosa.

Tarxien: Rural Traditions

Nestled in the heart of the Maltese countryside, Tarxien is a charming town that offers visitors a glimpse into the island's rural traditions and way of life. Far removed from the hustle and bustle of urban centres, Tarxien exudes a sense of tranquillity and authenticity, where time seems to move at a slower pace and the rhythms of rural life still hold sway.

As you wander through the streets of Tarxien, you'll be struck by the town's timeless charm and rustic beauty. Quaint stone houses with colourful wooden doors line the narrow lanes, while lush gardens and fruit trees dot the landscape, creating a picturesque backdrop for your exploration.

One of the highlights of Tarxien is its rich agricultural heritage, which dates back thousands of years to Malta's ancient past. The town is home to several traditional farms and vineyards, where local farmers tend to their crops and livestock using age-old techniques passed down through generations. Take a leisurely stroll through the fields and orchards, and you'll encounter rows of olive trees, grapevines heavy with fruit, and fields of golden wheat swaying in the breeze.

But perhaps the most iconic landmark in Tarxien is the Tarxien Temples, a UNESCO World Heritage Site that dates back over 5,000 years. These ancient megalithic structures are among the oldest freestanding stone buildings in the world, and offer a fascinating glimpse into Malta's prehistoric past. Wander through the labyrinthine chambers and corridors of the temples, and you'll encounter intricately carved stone altars, mysterious symbols, and awe-inspiring architectural feats that speak to the skill and ingenuity of their creators.

In addition to its archaeological wonders, Tarxien is also home to a vibrant community of artisans, craftsmen, and tradespeople, who keep alive the town's proud tradition of craftsmanship and creativity. Visit one of the local workshops or studios, and you'll find artisans hard at work crafting everything from handmade pottery and ceramics to intricate lace and textiles, each one a testament to Malta's rich cultural heritage.

As the sun sets over the tranquil countryside, Tarxien comes alive with the sounds of laughter and conversation, as locals gather in the town square to socialise and celebrate. Join in the festivities and immerse yourself in the warm hospitality of the Maltese people, as you sample traditional delicacies, sip on locally produced wine, and enjoy the company of newfound friends.

Whether you're a history enthusiast, a nature lover, or simply someone in search of a peaceful retreat, Tarxien offers a truly authentic Maltese experience that is sure to leave a lasting impression. So come and discover the rural traditions and timeless beauty of Tarxien, and experience the true essence of Malta's countryside.

St. Paul's Catacombs: Ancient Burial Grounds

Nestled beneath the bustling streets of Rabat, on the outskirts of Mdina, lies a hidden world that offers a glimpse into Malta's ancient past - the St. Paul's Catacombs. These underground burial grounds, carved out of solid rock over 1,500 years ago, are among the earliest and most extensive Christian catacombs in Malta, and offer visitors a fascinating insight into the island's early Christian history and funerary practices.

As you descend into the depths of the catacombs, you'll be struck by the eerie silence and darkness that envelops you, broken only by the faint flicker of candlelight and the occasional drip of water echoing through the chambers. Step inside, and you'll find yourself surrounded by a labyrinth of narrow passageways, winding tunnels, and hidden chambers, each one lined with rows of carved niches and burial alcoves.

Wander through the catacombs, and you'll encounter a wealth of archaeological treasures, from intricate frescoes and mosaics to elaborately carved sarcophagi and tombstones, each one bearing witness to the lives and beliefs of Malta's early Christian inhabitants. Explore the various levels and sections of the catacombs, and you'll discover a fascinating array of burial practices and rituals, from simple, unadorned graves to elaborate family tombs and communal ossuaries.

But perhaps the most remarkable feature of the St. Paul's Catacombs is their sheer size and complexity. Spread out over an area of over 2,000 square meters, the catacombs comprise a network of interconnected chambers and galleries, some of which extend to depths of over 10 meters below ground. It's believed that the catacombs were used not only as burial grounds, but also as meeting places for early Christian communities, who gathered here to worship, pray, and commemorate the lives of their loved ones.

In addition to their archaeological significance, the St. Paul's Catacombs also hold a special place in Maltese folklore and tradition. Legend has it that the catacombs are connected to the nearby Church of St. Paul's Grotto, where the apostle Paul is said to have taken refuge during his time in Malta. Whether or not this legend is true, the catacombs remain a place of pilgrimage and reverence for Christians around the world, who come here to pay their respects to the early martyrs and saints who lie buried within its ancient walls.

As you emerge from the depths of the catacombs and return to the surface world, you'll carry with you a newfound appreciation for Malta's rich cultural heritage and the enduring legacy of its early Christian communities. So come and explore the ancient burial grounds of St. Paul's Catacombs, and discover the secrets that lie hidden beneath the streets of Rabat.

Ghajn Tuffieha Bay: Hidden Gem

Nestled along the rugged coastline of Malta's northwest region lies a true hidden gem - Ghajn Tuffieha Bay. Tucked away from the crowds and commercialism that often accompany popular tourist spots, this pristine stretch of coastline offers visitors a tranquil escape into nature's embrace, where the azure waters meet the golden sands in perfect harmony.

As you make your way down the winding path that leads to Ghajn Tuffieha Bay, you'll feel a sense of anticipation building within you. The path meanders through lush Mediterranean vegetation, offering glimpses of the sparkling sea and rugged cliffs that lie beyond. With each step, the sound of the waves crashing against the shore grows louder, beckoning you closer to this hidden paradise.

And then, suddenly, the bay comes into view - a breathtaking panorama of natural beauty that takes your breath away. The crescent-shaped beach stretches out before you, framed by towering cliffs on either side, their rugged contours softened by the gentle embrace of vegetation. The crystal-clear waters of the Mediterranean glisten in the sunlight, inviting you to take a dip and cool off from the heat of the day.

As you set foot on the soft, golden sands of Ghajn Tuffieha Bay, you'll feel a sense of peace and serenity wash over you. Unlike some of Malta's more crowded beaches, this hidden gem offers plenty of space to spread out and relax, whether you're soaking up the sun on a beach towel, building sandcastles with the kids, or simply taking a leisurely stroll along the shoreline.

But Ghajn Tuffieha Bay isn't just about sun, sand, and sea - it's also a haven for nature lovers and outdoor enthusiasts. The surrounding countryside is crisscrossed with walking trails and hiking paths, offering spectacular views of the bay and the surrounding coastline. Take a leisurely hike up the nearby cliffs, and you'll be rewarded with panoramic vistas that stretch as far as the eye can see.

And if you're feeling adventurous, why not explore the nearby Gnejna Bay, a secluded cove just a short walk away from Ghajn Tuffieha Bay? This hidden gem offers all the beauty and tranquility of its sister beach, with the added bonus of even fewer crowds and more opportunities for snorkelling, swimming, and exploring.

As the sun begins to dip below the horizon, casting a warm, golden glow over the bay, you'll find yourself reluctant to leave this idyllic paradise behind. But as you make your way back up the winding path, you'll carry with you memories of a truly unforgettable day spent in the embrace of nature's beauty. So come and discover the hidden gem of Ghajn Tuffieha Bay, and experience the magic of Malta's northwest coast for yourself.

Inquisitor's Palace: Dark History Revealed

Standing proudly in the heart of Birgu, on the southeastern coast of Malta, the Inquisitor's Palace looms as a stark reminder of a dark chapter in the island's history. Built in the 16th century during the reign of the Knights of St. John, this imposing edifice served as the seat of the Maltese Inquisition for over 200 years, wielding power and authority over the lives of countless individuals deemed heretical or subversive.

Approaching the Inquisitor's Palace, visitors are immediately struck by its formidable presence. The imposing facade, with its austere stone walls and towering battlements, exudes an air of authority and foreboding, hinting at the secrets and horrors that lie within.

Step inside, and you'll find yourself transported back in time to a world of fear, suspicion, and oppression. The halls and chambers of the palace are steeped in history, with each room bearing witness to the trials and tribulations of those who fell afoul of the Inquisition's iron grip.

One of the most chilling aspects of the Inquisitor's Palace is its network of prison cells, where suspected heretics and dissenters were held captive and subjected to interrogation and torture. The dank, dimly-lit chambers serve as a stark reminder of the brutality and injustice that characterized the era of the Inquisition, leaving a haunting impression on all who dare to tread within.

But perhaps the most fascinating aspect of the Inquisitor's Palace is its collection of artefacts and exhibits, which offer a glimpse into the daily lives and practices of the Inquisition's agents and victims. From instruments of torture and punishment to religious relics and works of art, each item tells a story of faith, power, and persecution, shedding light on a dark and troubled period in Malta's past.

Despite its grim history, the Inquisitor's Palace is also a place of reflection and remembrance, where visitors can pay their respects to the countless individuals who suffered and died at the hands of the Inquisition. It serves as a sobering reminder of the importance of safeguarding freedom of thought and belief, and of remaining vigilant against the dangers of unchecked authority and intolerance.

As you leave the Inquisitor's Palace behind and step back out into the sunlight, you may find yourself pondering the lessons of the past and the legacy of injustice that still resonates today. But amidst the darkness, there is also hope - hope that by confronting and acknowledging our shared history, we can strive to build a more just and compassionate future for generations to come.

Birgu: Maritime Heritage

Nestled on the southeastern coast of Malta, overlooking the majestic Grand Harbour, lies the historic town of Birgu. With its rich maritime heritage and centuries-old charm, Birgu is a destination that beckons travellers to immerse themselves in its fascinating history and picturesque surroundings.

As you approach Birgu, you'll be greeted by its imposing fortifications, which stand as a testament to the town's strategic importance throughout the ages. Built by the Knights of St. John in the 16th century, these formidable walls once served as a bulwark against invaders, protecting the town and its inhabitants from countless sieges and attacks.

Step inside the walls of Birgu, and you'll find yourself transported back in time to a world of narrow cobblestone streets, historic palazzos, and quaint squares. The town's architecture reflects its diverse cultural heritage, with influences ranging from medieval Europe to the Arab world, creating a unique and captivating blend of styles.

One of the highlights of Birgu is its bustling waterfront, where colourful fishing boats bob gently in the harbour and waterfront cafes and restaurants invite visitors to relax and soak in the atmosphere. From here, you can catch a boat to nearby attractions such as the historic Fort St.

Angelo or the picturesque island of Vittoriosa, or simply sit back and watch the world go by.

But perhaps the most iconic landmark in Birgu is the Malta Maritime Museum, housed in the historic Old Naval Bakery. Here, you can explore exhibits detailing Malta's seafaring history, from the island's ancient maritime traditions to its pivotal role in the Mediterranean during the age of sail. Discover fascinating artefacts, models, and interactive displays that bring the story of Malta's maritime heritage to life, offering insight into the lives of sailors, fishermen, and shipbuilders throughout the ages.

As you wander through the streets of Birgu, you'll encounter other reminders of the town's maritime past, from historic shipyards and dockyards to charming seafront promenades and quaysides. Take a leisurely stroll along the waterfront, and you'll be rewarded with breathtaking views of the Grand Harbour and its bustling activity, as ships and boats come and go, carrying on the proud maritime tradition that has defined Birgu for centuries.

Whether you're a history enthusiast, an architecture buff, or simply someone in search of a picturesque seaside retreat, Birgu offers something for everyone. So come and explore the town's maritime heritage, and discover the timeless beauty and charm of this historic Maltese gem.

St. Agatha's Tower: Coastal Sentry

Perched proudly atop a rugged promontory overlooking the azure waters of the Mediterranean Sea, St. Agatha's Tower stands as a silent sentinel, guarding the northern shores of Malta with unwavering resolve. Also known as the Red Tower due to its distinctive hue, this imposing fortification is a testament to the island's rich military history and strategic importance throughout the ages.

As you approach St. Agatha's Tower, you can't help but be struck by its commanding presence against the backdrop of the rugged coastline. Built by the Knights of St. John in the late 17th century, the tower was part of a network of coastal defences designed to protect Malta from marauding pirates and invading forces.

Step inside the walls of St. Agatha's Tower, and you'll find yourself transported back in time to an era of cannons, muskets, and maritime warfare. The interior of the tower is a maze of narrow corridors, spiral staircases, and vaulted chambers, each one steeped in history and intrigue. Climb to the top of the tower, and you'll be rewarded with panoramic views of the surrounding countryside and coastline, stretching as far as the eye can see.

But St. Agatha's Tower isn't just about military history - it's also a place of natural beauty and tranquillity. The surrounding area is home to an abundance of native flora and fauna, making it a popular destination for nature lovers and outdoor enthusiasts. Take a leisurely hike along the coastal trails that wind their way around the tower, and you'll encounter breathtaking vistas, hidden coves, and secluded beaches that seem untouched by time.

In addition to its historical and natural attractions, St. Agatha's Tower also plays a vital role in Malta's cultural heritage. Throughout the year, the tower hosts a variety of events and activities, ranging from historical reenactments and military drills to art exhibitions and music performances. These events offer visitors a chance to immerse themselves in the rich tapestry of Maltese culture and traditions, while also enjoying the unique ambiance of this historic landmark.

As you explore the corridors and ramparts of St. Agatha's Tower, you can't help but feel a sense of awe and reverence for the generations of soldiers and sailors who once stood watch over Malta's shores. Their legacy lives on in the silent stones of the tower, a reminder of the island's resilience and determination in the face of adversity.

So come and experience the coastal sentry of St. Agatha's Tower for yourself, and discover the timeless beauty and history that lie hidden within its ancient walls.

Manoel Island: Natural Retreat

Nestled in the tranquil waters of Marsamxett Harbour, just off the coast of Valletta, lies a hidden oasis of natural beauty and serenity - Manoel Island. This picturesque islet, named after Grand Master Manuel de Vilhena who fortified it in the 18th century, offers visitors a peaceful retreat from the hustle and bustle of urban life, with its lush greenery, secluded beaches, and panoramic views of the surrounding harbour.

Approaching Manoel Island by boat, you'll be greeted by its rugged coastline and verdant landscape, which provide a stark contrast to the bustling cityscape of nearby Valletta. Stepping ashore, you'll find yourself enveloped in a sense of tranquillity and relaxation, as you wander along the winding paths and shaded groves that crisscross the island.

One of the highlights of Manoel Island is its natural beauty, which remains largely untouched by development. The island is home to a diverse array of flora and fauna, including native Mediterranean shrubs, trees, and wildflowers, as well as a variety of bird species that call the island home. Take a leisurely stroll through the island's lush gardens, and you'll encounter hidden pockets of beauty at every turn, from secluded glades and tranquil ponds to vibrant displays of seasonal blooms.

But Manoel Island isn't just about nature - it also boasts a rich cultural heritage that dates back centuries. The island is home to several historic landmarks, including the imposing Fort Manoel, which dominates the skyline with its imposing bastions and fortified walls. Built by the Knights of St. John in the 18th century, the fort served as a key defensive position during Malta's turbulent history, and today stands as a testament to the island's military prowess and architectural heritage.

In addition to its natural beauty and historical significance, Manoel Island also offers visitors a range of recreational activities and amenities to enjoy. The island is home to a marina, where visitors can moor their boats and yachts and explore the surrounding waters at their leisure. There are also several restaurants and cafes dotted along the waterfront, where you can enjoy a leisurely meal or refreshments while taking in the stunning views of the harbour.

Whether you're seeking a peaceful retreat in nature, a glimpse into Malta's storied past, or simply a place to relax and unwind, Manoel Island offers something for everyone. So come and discover the natural beauty and tranquillity of this hidden gem in the heart of Marsamxett Harbour, and experience the true essence of Maltese island life.

Ggantija Temples: Neolithic Marvels

Nestled on the idyllic island of Gozo, amidst the rolling hills and verdant countryside, lie the Ggantija Temples - a testament to the ingenuity and craftsmanship of Malta's ancient inhabitants. Dating back over 5,000 years, these remarkable megalithic structures are among the oldest free-standing temples in the world, predating the Pyramids of Egypt and Stonehenge.

Approaching the Ggantija Temples, visitors are immediately struck by their sheer size and scale. The two main temples, built from massive limestone blocks, stand as imposing monuments to the Neolithic people who constructed them. It's believed that these temples were dedicated to a fertility goddess, with their design and orientation thought to be aligned with astronomical phenomena such as the solstices and equinoxes.

Stepping inside the temples, visitors are transported back in time to a world of ritual and reverence. The interiors are adorned with intricate carvings and decorations, depicting symbols of fertility, abundance, and the natural world. Archaeological excavations have unearthed a wealth of artefacts, including pottery, tools, and religious figurines, offering insights into the daily lives and beliefs of Malta's ancient inhabitants.

But perhaps the most remarkable aspect of the Ggantija Temples is their construction. The sheer size and weight of the limestone blocks used in their construction are a testament to the skill and ingenuity of the Neolithic builders, who harnessed the power of simple tools and manpower to create these monumental structures. The temples are a testament to the engineering prowess of their creators, who managed to transport and erect these massive stones without the aid of modern technology.

In addition to their archaeological significance, the Ggantija Temples also hold a special place in Maltese folklore and tradition. Legend has it that the temples were built by a race of giants, who used their superhuman strength to move the massive stones into place. While the truth behind these myths may never be known, the temples continue to captivate the imagination of visitors from around the world, inspiring awe and wonder at the achievements of Malta's ancient ancestors.

As you explore the Ggantija Temples and ponder the mysteries of Malta's Neolithic past, you'll find yourself drawn into a world of ancient rituals, beliefs, and traditions. These megalithic marvels stand as a testament to the enduring legacy of Malta's ancient inhabitants, whose achievements continue to fascinate and inspire us to this day. So come and discover the wonders of the Ggantija Temples, and experience the magic of Malta's Neolithic heritage for yourself.

Valletta Waterfront: Modern Elegance

As the sun begins to dip below the horizon, casting a warm glow over the ancient city of Valletta, a new kind of beauty comes to life along the waterfront. The Valletta Waterfront, a modern marvel of architecture and design, stands as a testament to Malta's rich maritime heritage and its vibrant contemporary culture.

Approaching the Valletta Waterfront from the sea, visitors are greeted by a striking skyline of historic buildings and sleek, modern structures. The waterfront is a blend of old and new, with centuries-old warehouses and dockyards juxtaposed against sleek, glass-fronted restaurants and entertainment venues.

Stepping ashore, visitors find themselves immersed in a world of modern elegance and sophistication. The Valletta Waterfront is a bustling hub of activity, with a wide range of attractions and amenities to suit every taste and interest. From world-class restaurants and stylish cafes to trendy bars and chic boutiques, there's something here for everyone to enjoy.

But the Valletta Waterfront isn't just about dining and shopping - it's also a place to experience Malta's rich cultural heritage. The waterfront is home to a variety of cultural events and activities, including live music performances, art exhibitions, and theatrical productions. Visitors can immerse themselves in the vibrant atmosphere of Valletta's waterfront, surrounded by the sights and sounds of this historic city.

One of the highlights of the Valletta Waterfront is its stunning architecture. The waterfront is lined with beautifully restored buildings that once served as warehouses and storage facilities for Malta's bustling maritime trade. Today, these historic structures have been transformed into stylish restaurants, cafes, and shops, preserving their original charm while offering visitors a taste of modern luxury.

As night falls, the Valletta Waterfront takes on a magical atmosphere, with the twinkling lights of the city reflecting off the calm waters of the harbour. Visitors can enjoy a leisurely stroll along the waterfront promenade, taking in the breathtaking views of the city skyline and the majestic Grand Harbour beyond.

Whether you're looking for a romantic evening out, a day of shopping and dining, or simply a place to soak up the vibrant atmosphere of Malta's capital city, the Valletta Waterfront has something for everyone. So come and experience the modern elegance of this historic waterfront destination, and discover the magic of Valletta by the sea.

St. Julian's: Nightlife Hotspot

As dusk descends over the shimmering waters of St. Julian's Bay, the vibrant energy of Malta's nightlife begins to stir. Nestled along the bustling coastline just north of Valletta, St. Julian's emerges as a pulsating hub of entertainment, where locals and visitors alike come together to revel in the excitement of the night.

Approaching St. Julian's, you'll be greeted by a kaleidoscope of neon lights and bustling activity. The streets come alive with the sounds of laughter and music, as people spill out from lively bars and clubs, ready to embark on a night of unforgettable fun.

St. Julian's is renowned for its eclectic mix of nightlife options, catering to every taste and preference. From chic cocktail lounges and rooftop bars with panoramic views to high-energy nightclubs and beachfront parties, there's something here to suit every mood and occasion.

One of the most popular spots in St. Julian's is Paceville, a vibrant district known for its pulsating nightlife scene. Here, you'll find a dazzling array of bars, clubs, and late-night venues, where you can dance the night away to the latest beats spun by top DJs or enjoy a leisurely drink with friends in a stylish setting.

But St. Julian's isn't just about partying - it's also a place to indulge in world-class dining and entertainment. The waterfront promenade is lined with an array of restaurants, cafes, and eateries, offering everything from traditional Maltese cuisine to international delicacies. After dinner, you can catch a live music performance, stand-up comedy show, or theatre production at one of the many entertainment venues dotted throughout the area.

For those seeking a more laid-back evening, St. Julian's also offers plenty of options for relaxation and enjoyment. Take a leisurely stroll along the scenic waterfront, where you can admire the stunning views of the bay and watch the boats bobbing gently in the harbour. Or, head to one of the local beach clubs or lounges, where you can sip cocktails and soak up the Mediterranean sunshine in style.

As the night wears on, the energy of St. Julian's shows no signs of slowing down. Whether you're looking for a wild night out on the town or a more relaxed evening by the sea, St. Julian's has something for everyone. So come and experience the excitement of Malta's nightlife hotspot, and make memories that will last a lifetime.

Fort Rinella: Victorian Fortress

Perched on the southeastern coast of Malta, overlooking the picturesque Grand Harbour, stands a testament to the island's military history and engineering prowess - Fort Rinella. This imposing Victorian fortress, named after British Governor Sir William Reid, is a remarkable example of 19th-century military architecture and technology.

Approaching Fort Rinella, visitors are immediately struck by its commanding presence and formidable walls, which once served as a key defensive position for the British Empire. Built in the late 19th century to protect Malta's vital harbours from enemy attack, the fort is a symbol of the island's strategic importance during the Victorian era.

Stepping inside the walls of Fort Rinella, visitors are transported back in time to an era of colonial power and military might. The fort's interior is a maze of winding corridors, underground tunnels, and cavernous gun emplacements, each one steeped in history and intrigue. Here, you can explore the barracks, storerooms, and artillery positions that once housed soldiers and weaponry during times of conflict.

But perhaps the most impressive feature of Fort Rinella is its massive Armstrong gun, a colossal piece of artillery that was once the largest muzzle-loading gun in the world. Designed to defend Malta's harbours from the threat of enemy ships, this formidable weapon could hurl massive shells over great distances with deadly accuracy.

Visitors to Fort Rinella can witness the power and precision of the Armstrong gun in action during daily reenactments and demonstrations. Trained volunteers dressed in period costume bring the fort to life, showcasing the drills and techniques used by Victorian soldiers to operate the gun and defend Malta's shores.

In addition to its military significance, Fort Rinella also offers visitors a fascinating insight into daily life in a Victorian fortress. The fort's living history museum features exhibits on topics such as soldiering, Victorian engineering, and life on the home front, providing a comprehensive overview of this fascinating period in Malta's history.

As you explore Fort Rinella and immerse yourself in its rich heritage, you can't help but marvel at the ingenuity and determination of the people who built and defended this remarkable fortress. From its towering walls to its powerful guns, Fort Rinella stands as a testament to Malta's resilience and determination in the face of adversity. So come and discover the Victorian splendour of Fort Rinella, and experience the power and prestige of Malta's military past.

Xaghra: Village Charm

Nestled amidst the rolling hills and fertile valleys of Gozo lies the charming village of Xaghra, a hidden gem waiting to be discovered by discerning travellers seeking an authentic taste of Maltese life. With its quaint streets, rustic architecture, and welcoming atmosphere, Xaghra exudes a timeless charm that captures the hearts of all who visit.

Approaching Xaghra, you'll be greeted by the sight of traditional limestone houses adorned with colourful wooden balconies and vibrant bougainvillaea. The village square serves as the heart of Xaghra, bustling with activity as locals gather to socialise, shop at the weekly market, or enjoy a leisurely meal at one of the charming cafes or restaurants that line the streets.

Wandering through the narrow lanes and alleyways of Xaghra, you'll discover hidden treasures at every turn. The village is home to a number of historic landmarks, including the majestic Xaghra Parish Church, dedicated to the Nativity of Our Lady. With its imposing facade and ornate interior, the church is a testament to the village's strong religious heritage and architectural legacy.

But Xaghra isn't just about history and culture - it's also a place to connect with nature and explore the island's natural beauty. Just a short distance from the village lies the breathtaking Ramla Bay, known for its golden sands, crystal-clear waters, and stunning views of the surrounding countryside. Whether you're soaking up the sun on the beach or embarking on a scenic hike along the coastal trails, Ramla Bay offers endless opportunities for outdoor adventure and relaxation.

Back in the village, visitors can immerse themselves in the local way of life by participating in traditional activities such as breadmaking, wine tasting, or pottery workshops. Xaghra is also known for its vibrant cultural events and festivals, which celebrate everything from music and dance to food and folklore, providing a unique opportunity to experience the rich tapestry of Maltese culture.

As the sun sets over the village, casting a warm glow over its limestone facades, you'll find yourself enchanted by the timeless beauty and village charm of Xaghra. Whether you're exploring its historic landmarks, enjoying its natural wonders, or simply soaking up the laid-back atmosphere, Xaghra offers a truly unforgettable experience that will leave you longing to return again and again.

Ta' Pinu Basilica: Spiritual Sanctuary

Nestled amidst the gentle hills and picturesque countryside of Gozo stands the Ta' Pinu Basilica, a spiritual sanctuary that draws pilgrims and visitors from around the world seeking solace, reflection, and divine intervention. Perched on a hilltop overlooking the quaint village of Għarb, this majestic basilica holds a special place in the hearts of the Maltese people and serves as a beacon of faith and devotion.

Approaching Ta' Pinu Basilica, visitors are struck by its imposing presence and striking architectural beauty. The basilica's imposing facade, adorned with intricate stone carvings and ornate sculptures, is a testament to the skill and craftsmanship of its builders. Stepping inside, visitors are enveloped in a sense of peace and tranquillity, as shafts of sunlight filter through the stained glass windows, casting a warm glow over the interior.

The origins of Ta' Pinu Basilica date back to the late 19th century when a humble chapel stood on the site. According to legend, a local woman claimed to have witnessed a series of miraculous events at the chapel, including the appearance of the Virgin Mary herself. In response to these divine manifestations, the chapel was expanded and transformed into the magnificent basilica that stands today, a testament to the enduring power of faith and devotion.

Today, Ta' Pinu Basilica serves as a place of pilgrimage and prayer for Catholics and non-Catholics alike. The basilica is home to a number of revered relics and religious artifacts, including a statue of the Virgin Mary that is said to have miraculous healing powers. Visitors come from far and wide to pay their respects, offer prayers, and seek comfort in the presence of the divine.

But Ta' Pinu Basilica is more than just a place of worship - it's also a symbol of hope and healing for those facing adversity or hardship. The basilica's tranquil surroundings and serene atmosphere provide a sanctuary for reflection and contemplation, offering solace to those in need of spiritual guidance or support.

As you explore Ta' Pinu Basilica and immerse yourself in its rich history and heritage, you'll be captivated by the sense of reverence and awe that permeates this sacred space. Whether you're seeking solace, inspiration, or simply a moment of quiet reflection, Ta' Pinu Basilica offers a haven of peace and tranquillity amidst the hustle and bustle of everyday life.

Fortifications Interpretation Centre: Military Legacy

Nestled within the historic walls of Valletta, the Fortifications Interpretation Centre stands as a testament to Malta's rich military legacy and its strategic importance throughout the centuries. Perched on the edge of the Grand Harbour, this unique museum offers visitors a fascinating insight into the island's fortifications and the role they played in shaping its history.

Approaching the Fortifications Interpretation Centre, visitors are greeted by the sight of imposing stone walls and bastions that have stood the test of time. These fortifications, built by the Knights of St. John and later expanded by the British, served as a vital line of defence for Malta against invading forces and naval attacks.

Stepping inside the museum, visitors are transported back in time to a bygone era of warfare and conquest. The exhibits showcase the evolution of Malta's fortifications, from the medieval period to the modern era, highlighting the innovative techniques and strategic planning that went into their construction.

One of the highlights of the Fortifications Interpretation Centre is its collection of artefacts and memorabilia related to Malta's military history. From ancient weapons and armour to intricate models and maps, these displays offer a glimpse into the daily lives of the soldiers who defended the island against foreign invaders.

But the museum isn't just about showcasing the past - it's also about educating and inspiring future generations about the importance of preserving Malta's cultural heritage. Interactive exhibits and multimedia presentations bring the history of Malta's fortifications to life, allowing visitors to immerse themselves in the sights and sounds of battle.

As you explore the Fortifications Interpretation Centre, you'll gain a newfound appreciation for the strategic significance of Malta's fortifications and the ingenuity of the people who built them. Whether you're a history buff, a military enthusiast, or simply curious about the island's rich heritage, the museum offers a captivating journey through time that is sure to leave a lasting impression.

Tarxien Rainbows: Natural Phenomenon

In the heart of the Mediterranean, on the sun-kissed island of Malta, lies a natural wonder that captivates the imagination and stirs the soul - the Tarxien Rainbows. Nestled amidst the rugged landscape of the southern coast, these mesmerising arcs of colour paint the sky in a breathtaking display of beauty and magic.

Approaching Tarxien, visitors are greeted by the sight of rolling countryside, dotted with quaint villages and ancient ruins. But it's when the sun begins to set that the real spectacle unfolds. As the golden rays of dusk give way to twilight, the sky comes alive with vibrant hues of red, orange, yellow, green, blue, indigo, and violet, forming a dazzling rainbow that stretches across the horizon.

The phenomenon of the Tarxien Rainbows occurs when the setting sun's rays pass through a veil of mist or rain, creating a prism effect that disperses light into its component colours. The result is a breathtaking display of colour and light that seems almost otherworldly in its beauty.

Locals and visitors alike gather at vantage points along the southern coast to witness this natural spectacle, cameras poised to capture the fleeting moment of magic. Whether you're watching from the cliffs overlooking the sea or from the comfort of a seaside cafe, the Tarxien Rainbows never fail to inspire awe and wonder.

But the magic of the Tarxien Rainbows isn't just limited to the evening hours. On clear mornings, early risers are treated to the sight of dew-kissed fields and meadows bathed in the soft glow of dawn, with rainbows arching gracefully overhead. It's a reminder of the beauty and resilience of nature, and a testament to the island's unique charm.

As you stand beneath the Tarxien Rainbows, surrounded by the beauty of Malta's southern coast, you can't help but feel a sense of wonder and gratitude for the natural world. It's a moment of pure magic, a fleeting glimpse of the extraordinary beauty that lies just beyond the horizon. So come and experience the Tarxien Rainbows for yourself, and let yourself be enchanted by the wonders of nature.

Grandmaster's Palace: Historical Splendor

In the heart of Malta's capital city, Valletta, stands a magnificent testament to the island's rich history and grandeur - the Grandmaster's Palace. This iconic landmark, with its imposing facade and opulent interiors, serves as a reminder of Malta's illustrious past as a strategic stronghold of the Mediterranean.

Approaching the Grandmaster's Palace, visitors are immediately struck by its grandeur and architectural beauty. Built in the 16th century as the official residence of the Grand Master of the Knights of St. John, the palace boasts a striking Baroque facade adorned with intricate carvings and decorative features.

Stepping through the palace gates, visitors are transported back in time to an era of royal splendor and noble extravagance. The interior of the palace is a treasure trove of art and history, with lavish rooms adorned with priceless tapestries, frescoes, and antique furnishings.

One of the highlights of the Grandmaster's Palace is the State Rooms, which served as the official residence of the Grand Master and his retinue. Here, visitors can admire the grandeur of the Council Chamber, where important meetings and ceremonies took place, as well as the lavish State Apartments, which were used for entertaining foreign dignitaries and nobility.

But the Grandmaster's Palace is more than just a symbol of wealth and power - it also holds a special place in Malta's collective memory as a site of resistance and resilience. During the Great Siege of Malta in 1565, the palace served as a stronghold against the invading Ottoman forces, with its fortified walls and strategic position overlooking the Grand Harbour.

Today, the Grandmaster's Palace serves as the seat of the President of Malta and houses the Office of the President, as well as the Parliament of Malta. It also serves as a museum, showcasing a wealth of artifacts and exhibits that illuminate Malta's rich cultural heritage and political history.

As you explore the Grandmaster's Palace and immerse yourself in its grandeur and splendor, you'll gain a newfound appreciation for Malta's storied past and the legacy of the Knights of St. John. Whether you're a history enthusiast, an art lover, or simply curious about the island's rich heritage, the Grandmaster's Palace offers a captivating journey through time that is sure to leave a lasting impression.

Zurrieq: Rustic Beauty

Nestled in the southwestern region of Malta, amid rolling countryside and picturesque landscapes, lies the charming village of Zurrieq. Steeped in rustic beauty and tranquil charm, Zurrieq offers visitors a glimpse into traditional Maltese life and a chance to escape the hustle and bustle of modernity.

Approaching Zurrieq, visitors are greeted by the sight of quaint limestone buildings adorned with colourful wooden balconies and blooming flower boxes. The village exudes an atmosphere of peaceful serenity, with narrow winding streets and hidden alleyways waiting to be explored.

As you wander through Zurrieq, you'll discover hidden treasures at every turn. The village is home to a number of historic landmarks and cultural attractions, including the stunning Parish Church of St. Catherine, with its ornate facade and majestic bell tower. Inside, visitors can admire the intricate frescoes and Baroque architecture that adorn the interior, offering a glimpse into Malta's rich religious heritage.

But Zurrieq isn't just about history and architecture - it's also a place to connect with nature and enjoy the great outdoors. The village is surrounded by lush countryside and fertile valleys, making it the perfect destination for hiking, cycling, and exploring the scenic beauty of the Maltese landscape.

One of the highlights of Zurrieq is the Blue Grotto, a series of sea caves and natural rock formations that dot the coastline. Visitors can take a boat tour to explore these mystical caverns and marvel at the crystal-clear waters and vibrant marine life that inhabit them.

Back in the village, visitors can immerse themselves in the local way of life by sampling traditional Maltese cuisine at one of the charming cafes or tavernas that line the streets. From hearty stews and fresh seafood to sweet pastries and locally produced wine, Zurrieq offers a taste of authentic Maltese hospitality.

As the sun sets over Zurrieq, casting a warm glow over its rustic streets and countryside, you'll find yourself enchanted by the timeless beauty and village charm of this hidden gem. Whether you're exploring its historic landmarks, enjoying its natural wonders, or simply soaking up the laid-back atmosphere, Zurrieq offers a truly authentic Maltese experience that will leave you longing to return again and again.

San Anton Gardens: Botanical Delights

Nestled in the heart of the idyllic village of Attard, on the Mediterranean island of Malta, lies a verdant oasis of tranquillity and beauty - the San Anton Gardens. These historic gardens, dating back to the 17th century, are a botanical paradise that delights visitors with their lush greenery, colourful blooms, and serene atmosphere.

As you step through the gates of San Anton Gardens, you are immediately enveloped in a sense of peace and serenity. The air is filled with the sweet fragrance of flowers, and the sound of birdsong fills the air, creating a symphony of nature that soothes the soul.

Wandering along the winding pathways of the gardens, visitors are treated to a feast for the senses at every turn. Towering palm trees, majestic cypress trees, and fragrant citrus groves provide shade and shelter, while vibrant flower beds burst with a riot of colour, from delicate roses and cheerful daisies to exotic orchids and aromatic herbs.

One of the highlights of San Anton Gardens is the beautifully landscaped lawns and formal gardens, which are meticulously maintained and showcase a variety of rare and exotic plant species. The gardens are also home to several charming fountains, statues, and ornamental features, adding to the sense of elegance and refinement.

But San Anton Gardens is not just a place of beauty - it is also steeped in history and culture. The gardens are located within the grounds of the historic San Anton Palace, which has served as the official residence of the President of Malta since 1974. Visitors can explore the palace's ornate interiors and learn about its fascinating history, which dates back to the time of the Knights of St. John.

Whether you're a nature lover, a history buff, or simply looking for a peaceful retreat from the hustle and bustle of everyday life, San Anton Gardens offers something for everyone. So take a leisurely stroll through its verdant pathways, breathe in the fragrant air, and immerse yourself in the beauty and tranquillity of this botanical paradise.

The Malta Aviation Museum: Flying Through History

Nestled on the outskirts of the quaint village of Ta' Qali, amidst the rugged Maltese countryside, lies a treasure trove of aviation history - the Malta Aviation Museum. This fascinating museum offers visitors a unique opportunity to delve into the rich and storied past of aviation in Malta, from its humble beginnings to its pivotal role in World War II and beyond.

As you approach the Malta Aviation Museum, you're greeted by the sight of vintage aircraft parked on the tarmac, their sleek silhouettes standing in stark contrast to the azure skies above. Stepping inside the museum, you're immediately struck by the sense of awe and wonder as you're surrounded by a collection of meticulously restored aircraft, artifacts, and exhibits that showcase the evolution of aviation in Malta.

The museum's extensive collection includes a wide range of aircraft, from iconic Spitfires and Hurricanes to historic biplanes and helicopters. Each aircraft tells a story, offering a glimpse into the bravery and ingenuity of the pilots who flew them and the crucial role they played in shaping Malta's history.

105

One of the highlights of the Malta Aviation Museum is its comprehensive collection of World War II aircraft, which pays tribute to Malta's role as the "unsinkable aircraft carrier" during the Siege of Malta. Visitors can marvel at the Spitfires and Hurricanes that defended the island against relentless enemy attacks, and learn about the heroic efforts of the pilots who fought valiantly to protect Malta's skies.

But the museum's exhibits go beyond just military aircraft - they also explore the civilian side of aviation, showcasing the evolution of commercial aviation in Malta and the pioneering spirit of the island's aviators. From early flying boats and seaplanes to modern airliners and helicopters, the museum offers a comprehensive overview of Malta's aviation heritage.

As you explore the Malta Aviation Museum and immerse yourself in its rich history and heritage, you can't help but feel a sense of admiration for the men and women who took to the skies and paved the way for the future of flight. Whether you're a history enthusiast, an aviation buff, or simply curious about Malta's fascinating past, the Malta Aviation Museum offers a captivating journey through time that is sure to leave a lasting impression.

Afterword

As our journey through the captivating wonders of Malta draws to a close, it's time to reflect on the experiences we've shared and the memories we've made along the way. From the historic streets of Valletta to the tranquil shores of Gozo, from the ancient temples of Tarxien to the natural splendor of the Blue Grotto, Malta has enchanted us with its beauty, history, and culture at every turn.

Throughout our exploration of this remarkable island, we've encountered a tapestry of sights, sounds, and sensations that have left an indelible mark on our hearts and minds. We've marveled at the grandeur of Valletta's baroque architecture, wandered through the silent streets of Mdina, and soaked up the sun on the sandy shores of Golden Bay. We've tasted the flavors of Maltese cuisine, explored the depths of ancient caves, and soared through the skies at the Malta Aviation Museum.

But beyond the attractions and landmarks, it's the people of Malta who have truly made our journey unforgettable. From the warm hospitality of the locals to the passionate guides who have shared their knowledge and stories with us, we've been welcomed with open arms and treated like family every step of the way.

As we bid farewell to Malta, let us carry with us the memories of our adventures and the lessons we've learned along the way. Let us remember the resilience of the Maltese people, who have overcome countless challenges throughout history to emerge stronger and more vibrant than ever. And let us cherish the beauty of this magical island, with its rich tapestry of history, culture, and natural wonders, knowing that we carry a piece of Malta with us wherever we go.

So until we meet again, may your travels be filled with adventure, discovery, and the joy of new experiences. And may Malta always hold a special place in your heart, as it does in ours. Safe travels, and may the spirit of Malta guide you wherever you roam.

Made in United States
Orlando, FL
11 November 2024

53745456R00065